Lessons of
Hope & Resilience

A PARENT/TEACHER GUIDE FOR THE STORY, "A RIVER'S JOURNEY"

Nancy T. Cupolo

DISCLAIMER

The information, presented by the author in this book, represents over forty-five years of experience as an educator, professor, training specialist, and consultant. It is intended solely as information sharing and should not be construed as advice from a licensed professional.

The author or illustrator assume no responsibility or liability, and should not be held accountable or responsible for the use of the information contained herein.

The ideas presented, by the author, based upon a strong knowledge base in child development and curriculum development does not preclude the parent, teacher, or reader from seeking the advice of a licensed professional. The author encourages the parent, teacher, and/or reader to do so.

Illustrations by Lisa M. Cupolo
Book design by The Troy Book Makers

Printed in the United States of America
The Troy Book Makers • Troy, New York • thetroybookmakers.com

To order additional copies of this title,
contact your favorite local bookstore
or visit www.shoptbmbooks.com

ISBN: 978-1-61468-803-7

Lessons of Hope & Resilience

A PARENT/TEACHER GUIDE FOR THE STORY, "A RIVER'S JOURNEY"

This guide is a collection of practical ideas and teaching strategies
for parents and teachers that will enhance learning,
extend a child's thinking, and reinforce the child's innate curiosity
about the beauty of nature and the world.

Written by

Nancy T. Cupolo

Illustrated by

Lisa M. Cupolo

Dedication

*To my parents George & Alice Burke, my first teachers,
who taught me to be resilient, hopeful, faith- filled,
and to always "do good" in this world!*

*To my sister, Carol Jean (Beanie,)
who at the young age of eleven, just before she died,
taught me to cherish the beauty that surrounds us
and the love that is in our heart each and every day.*

*To Stuart Pixley, who, at the early age of four,
inspired me to become a teacher.*

*To teachers and parents everywhere
who encourage children every day to
think, dream, and believe!*

BUTTERFLY WISH

In its metamorphosis from the common caterpillar to a beautiful butterfly, the butterfly gives us hope. The butterfly has become a symbol of transformation and resilience across cultures. It demonstrates growth and new beginnings. In the story, "A River's Journey", the butterfly signifies the power in each one of us to transform ourselves and to overcome obstacles in our everyday lives.

The river represents strength. We all have the ability to persevere through difficult times, and emerge better and stronger than before.

This guide is a collection of practical ideas and lesson plans for parents and teachers that will enhance learning, extend a child's thinking, and instill curiosity about the beauty of nature.

This story guide provides strategies and ideas for lessons in hope and resilience which are much needed in our troubled world.

It is important that we always give our children hope and teach them how to become resilient.

Contents

Introduction

As a parent, you are your child's first teacher. When your child came into this world you were the first person that he/she saw. You were the first person to hold, cuddle, and smile at your beautiful baby. You were the first one to speak to your child, and perhaps the first one to tell him/her a story.

As a teacher, you are "on the front line". You are one of the first adults, outside of the home, who spends endless hours guiding young children in their cognitive, physical, and social emotional development. In unity with the parents, you help to neuro-network the synapses of the child's brain. There is no other more noble a profession than being a parent or teacher! What you say and do impacts the child for life!

Seize the teachable moments of childhood! Enjoy countless hours of reading **with** your children as you instill a passion for learning that extends well beyond the confines of a book.

"A River's Journey" is a beautifully illustrated and imaginative story about the magic of nature from the river's view. However, the story does not stop there! The story continues in the mind and heart of the reader. The story of the river's journey lives on in each one of us as we draw, write, read, explore, and discover.

The story presents a wonderful opportunity for continued discovery and wonder about the world around us. It is simply a **springboard** for discussion and an **exploration** in learning.

As a teacher, or parent, you possess the tremendous power to encourage your child to wonder about his/her world. You have the ability to instill, in the child, a lifelong curiosity for learning and a love of nature.

As parents and teachers we inspire dreams and change lives. We have the potential to help our children see the beauty in our world and to teach them how to cherish and protect the environment in which they live.

This publication, "Lessons of Hope & Resilience: A Parent/ Teacher Guide for the story, "A River's Journey", provides ideas and strategies to extend the child's learning beyond the story itself.

Children are multi-modality learners who need to touch, see, hear, and move in order to learn.

The information contained in this guide is simply that, "a guide" that will enhance lessons and interactions with children in a sensorial and fun manner.

It is important to recognize the significance of story telling as a life-long skill for the young and old alike. As a child's "first teacher" it is imperative that you understand the drawing, writing, reading connection that begins with a child's scribbles at eighteen months of age.

This guide discusses the inherent constructs in the drawing, writing and reading process. It also provides some concrete ideas and strategies for young children that will extend their thinking, their passion for learning, and their love of nature. Let's begin our journey together with the river!

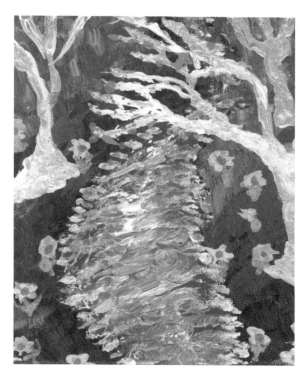

THE RIVER

The river is a path that depicts the beginnings of life. The meeting of the river with the ocean symbolizes the end of life. Life is like a river. It can flow slowly or it can flow quickly, it can change course, however nothing can stop the river from flowing. So too are our children, learning at their own pace, ever changing, ever growing and always moving forward in life.

Our lessons must reflect this.

The Importance of Story-telling

If a child can "tell a story", in his/her own words, or express their thoughts and ideas in a drawing, no matter how primitive the drawing is, he/she will be able to bring beauty into our world. If a child believes that their "work" is important and beautiful he/she will be motivated to draw, write, and read as an expression of his/her emotions and feelings.

Storytelling originated with visual stories, an example of this is cave drawings. Storytelling shifted to oral traditions, in which stories were passed down from generation to generation by word of mouth. As time went by the words formed into narratives, including written, printed, and typed stories.

The earliest forms of storytelling were usually spoken. The storyteller would use gestures and role-playing to get their point across in an often descriptive and animated fashion.

Stories were created to pass down family traditions. Story-telling was a medium that was used to share the history of the family with younger people. Stories also were used to teach children basic life lessons in storytelling form. For example, the story of Hansel and Gretel was meant to warn children about the dangers of wandering into the woods on their own.

Effective storytellers have the ability to captivate their audience, leave the listener/reader with new knowledge and an insatiable curiosity to learn more. This new knowledge and heightened curiosity is something that they may carry with them for the rest of their lives.

Good stories are easy to understand. They are also told in a language that young children can relate to. Simple stories are easy for children to remember. "A River's Journey" is a simple story that has multiple meanings.

Before reading, "A River's Journey", encourage children to tell stories or create scribbles/drawings of how they feel or what they see around them. Keep in mind that each child's learning modality is different. One child may like to tell a story, another child may like to sing a story, while another child may like to draw a story.

Begin by supplying children with the tools and equipment that they need in order to express their emotions, thoughts, and ideas in their own unique way. Some of these tools may include:

- Crayons, paper, chalk, a chalk board.

- A wipe off board, magic markers.

- Paints, paint brushes, an easel.

- A bucket of water and various size paint brushes for outside art/drawing/writings on the pavement.

- Sponges/gadgets to paint with.

- A musical instrument, a song.

- A place to dance.

- A puppet.

As you begin to tell a story, or encourage the child to tell a story, be mindful that the young child has to be able to interact with the story. He/she needs to see concrete props that illustrate the story. For "A River's Journey" you might begin by allowing a pretend lady bug (a puppet) to crawl up and down your arm as you sing a song about a lady bug. Ask the children to look for the lady bug in the book as the story is read to them. This is called an anticipatory set. An anticipatory set provides children with a focal point prior to reading the story.

As the story develops and is shared with the children it is important to:

- Engage/immerse the child in the story.

- Relate the story to their personal lives.

- Create suspense using the element of surprise.

- Bring the characters/illustrations to life.

- Use demonstrations throughout the story.

- Encourage the child to use their hands and body to express the story.

- "Sing" the story.

- Ask open ended questions. "What does the river see? Look up two love doves kissing in a _____ (tree)."

LOVE DOVES

Doves symbolize peace, freedom, and love.
Allow the children to be free to express themselves in unique ways.

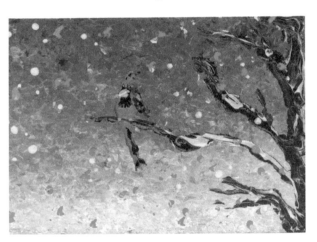

THE CARDINAL

The cardinal symbolizes a loved one who has passed away. Some believe that the bird is their loved one, returning for a visit. Cardinals represent devotion. In Native American lore, some tribes thought that the cardinal brought rain, and the sun.

Create a play or skit about the cardinal, the rain, and sunshine in order to make the story come alive!

SHOOTING STAR

A shooting star symbolizes good luck and positivity. Allow the children to move/dance like a star or make a wish upon a star. Become little scientists and investigate how stars are formed.

FIND YOUR SPARK

Fire is a symbol of light, warmth, energy, and inspiration. Encourage children to find their own spark.

Helpful Hints While Reading *With* Children

The most avid of readers were storytellers first! Sometimes we have a tendency to read "**TO**" children instead of reading "**WITH**" children. When presenting the story of, "A River's Journey", it is important to allow the child to anticipate what the story may be about. He/she should be allowed to express his/her ideas and opinions as the book is presented. Once the ideas have been expressed, by the children and written down, you can begin by sharing the title and contents of the story. The contents can be shown in visual format first in order to establish a purpose for reading.

Survey the cover of the book with the children and ask them to predict what they think the story may be about. Identify and discuss the difficult words, phrases, and concepts in the book briefly. Identify the author and illustrator's names. Follow up after reading the story to encourage the children to think, talk, draw and write about the topics/paintings that are presented in the text.

Even if the children, that you are with, can read on their own, there is value in reading aloud with them. A child's listening skills are usually stronger than his/her reading skills. A child can comprehend more if he/she reads along silently as you read the book out loud.

Let the children tell you the story first, the content can be what they imagine it to be from the paintings/visuals. When you read, read short passages, and extend the reading time if the children can stay focused.

Engage the imagination. As the child reads or listens, encourage him/her to visualize the events in the story, creating a picture or movie in his/her mind. After a few pages, ask him/her to describe the story in his/her own words. Visual imagery is a powerful teaching tool.

FOOTPRINTS IN THE SNOW

Is the river made of rain and snow?
Look close, soft, quiet footprints in the snow. Where do they go?

When reading a book with a child, stop occasionally to ask what he/she thinks might happen next. This requires him/ her to integrate what he/she has learned so far and predict what will happen next. Engage the child in a discussion surrounding his/her favorite part of the story or favorite illustration.

Encourage children to extend the story by drawing or adding words or a script for older children who can already write. The story should become an *interactive experience*. It is ok if the children are not sitting perfectly still.

*We learn best within a social context by hearing
and then sharing what we are experiencing!*

The Drawing, Writing, Reading Connection

Learning is a life- long process. Literacy does not begin at a certain point in a child's life, rather it is a continuous process of learning. A child's reading begins with basic scribbling and evolves into emergent drawing, writing, and reading. Exposure to literature at an early age can and does help children to become good readers later in life.

All children scribble using twenty basic scribbles. (these scribbles are common scribbles world-wide). The scribbles form symbols and shapes that begin to evolve into a mandala that looks like a sun. The symbol of the sun transforms into the face of a person as children scribble on.

The two-year-old doesn't start out with a plan in mind but when she looks at a scribble after it is finished, she sees a visual whole and entity. The child's view is illustrated perfectly in the answer of this little girl when her teacher asked, "What are you drawing?". The little girl explained it all when she responded. "How do I know until I have finished?".

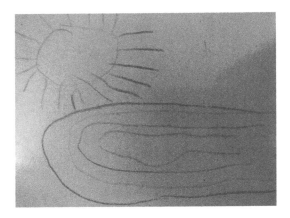

Mandalas are depicted early in children's drawings they look like the sun. The child then proceeds to draw suns, radials, and eventually human figures.

The child's first drawing of human figures look very strange to adults. The body is usually round. The arms sprout out from the head. When the child draws this creation he/she does not care whether the picture looks like people. It is simply a variation on a design of shapes, lines, circles, and triangles.

The child's symbols become a story.
The symbols begin to merge as letters of the alphabet.
The letters become words, the words become writing,
and the writing becomes reading.

When a child draws, they communicate an idea through visual symbols. When they write, they communicate through the symbols of letters. This is a multi-modality approach to learning that is instinctive to a young child. Children can express themselves through images that they draw, then stringing letters together to create words, and gradually invented spelling and writing.

When a child draws, he/she is telling a story. The child becomes a writer the first time that he/she scribbles with a crayon. Sometimes this happens as early as eighteen months of age.

Drawing helps a child remember things around them. The child is provided the opportunity to process information in multiple ways: visually, kinesthetically(through movement), and tactually when he/she draws.

The beginning stages of the drawing, writing, and reading connection are:

- Stage 1: Random Scribbling (15 months to 2 1/2 years)

- Stage 2: Controlled Scribbling (2 years to 3 years)

- Stage 3: Lines and Patterns (2 1/2 years to 3 1/2 years)

- Stage 4: Pictures of Objects or People (3 years to 5 years)

Stage 6: Symbols and Letters (3years to six years)

Stage 7: Letters and words (4years to six years)

Drawing guides children in thinking, organizing their own ideas, and then writing about them.

Children should be encouraged to draw pictures about the story that they hear or read to improve their reading comprehension. Drawing will also motivate children to read more!

The writing process develops as the drawing process continues. Drawing and writing are connected as follows:

- Scribbling.

- Drawing. Using a variety of mediums children draw pictures of familiar places and objects.

- Creating letter-like shapes.

- Reproducing strings of random letters. (known as the re-occurring principle in art)

- Invented/Transitional Spelling.

- Standard Spelling.

FINGERPRINTS AND A SNOW MOBILE.

DRAWING FAMILIAR PLACES AND OBJECTS.

MOM, DAD, NANCY, AND FRANK.

INVENTED SPELLING.

The reading process emerges along with the writing process. Reading is the process of making meaning from print. Children begin to identify the words in print. This is called word recognition. Next, they begin to construct meanings from the words. This is called comprehension.

Children go through four stages of reading development: emergent reading, early reading, transitional reading, and fluent reading. Although the order of the stages remains the same, children progress through these stages at different rates.

The reading process evolves in five stages:

- Prereading.

- Reading.

- Responding.

- Exploring.

- Applying.

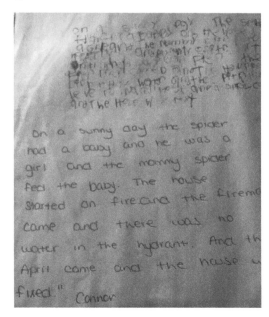

APPLYING

MAKING MEANING FROM PRINT.

Children begin to represent the world around them in their drawings. They begin to write down their "story" in personally meaningful ways.

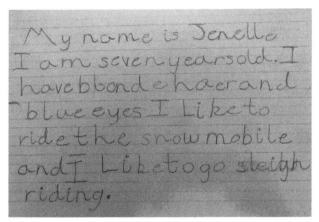

To improve children's comprehension when reading you can:

- Have them read aloud. Let the child record their voice while reading.

- Reread the story to build fluency.

- Supplement their reading with other stories about the river, birds, trees etc.

- ✳ Talk about what they're reading.

- ✳ Encourage them to form visual images of the story content in their mind.

- ✳ Add interesting facts about the story content.

Some examples of "interesting facts" that can be derived from the illustrations in the story, A River's Journey are:

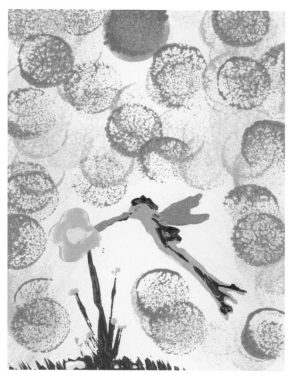

THE HUMMING BIRD

A Humming Bird symbolizes intelligence, beauty, devotion, love and good luck. These birds are also respected as defenders of their territory. Humming birds are only a few inches long. Humming birds flap their wings so fast they create an actual humming sound that gives them their name. They are smart because they can remember every flower that they have visited.

RIVER TRAVELER

The river itself is a path. As the river flows along so does the beauty it brings to each river bank side. The river may be different colors, such as blue, muddy brown and even black. The river has meanders, curves along it's path.

SILVER LINING

Rainbows are multi-colored arcs that form in the sky and are created when sunlight shines through the water. As a result, light reflects off the water droplets, bends (called refraction) and splits. When sunlight shines through the water droplets, it splits into seven colors.

NANCY T. CUPOLO

A Sample Lesson Plan for Young Children

The story teller or reader has less than two minutes to captivate his/her audience! The most important part of any lesson is the introduction. Children are movers and shakers. They are sensory creatures who like to touch, sing, dance, and interact with what they are learning. It is imperative then to incorporate each child's learning modality into the lesson in order to captivate their interest. Start with a song, a concrete prop, and some movement before you begin reading the story together.

There are several components in every lesson that you should keep in mind as you interact with young children such as:

- **The introduction**: use a concrete prop (perhaps a lady bug puppet) .

- **Anticipatory set**: sing a song about a lady bug (a reflection of the painting in the book) that allows children to move like a lady bug and anticipate seeing a lady bug in the story.

- **Recording children's ideas:** using a KWL chart write down the child's ideas: (K)What do you know about a river? (W) What do you want to learn about a river? (L) What have you learned about a river after reading the story?

- **Story prediction**: examine the cover of the book with the children and ask them to predict what the story might be about.

- **Story telling/reading:** use inflection in your voice & animation on your face.

- **Re-telling the Story:** let the children re-tell the story.

- **The culmination:** Summarize key points in the story: Will the river empty into the sea? Or will all of it's goodness stay forever with you and me?

- **Story questions**: Who? What? When? How did the story end?

- **A story extension**: allow the child (children) to change the story ending. Draw how they feel upon completion of the story. Create a skit about the story. Write down things that they want to know more about.

Keep in mind that children who live in poverty may speak in circular discourse (the story goes around and around, and never seems to end) while children who live in the middle class may speak in linear discourse (the story has a beginning, a middle and an end). Some children may need additional assistance with identifying the story content in a linear fashion, however those who speak in circular discourse are often the best of story tellers!

Every child has strengths that contribute to the story!

Several story props are represented in the story itself. The props used to enhance the story can be three dimensional representations of the object or a photo of the object.

Prop ideas that are illustrated in the story include: A lady bug, tulips, a daisy, a heart, doves, snow prints, a cardinal, the sun, trees, a waterfall, a humming bird, dandelions, a butterfly, a rain bow, a fire, stars, ice, snow, and a cherry blossom tree.

FOLLOW YOUR FAITH FILLED HEART

The ladybug symbolizes resilience, protection, healing, luck, and grace. The lady bug protects plants and flowers from pests and other bugs.

ANGEL FALLS

Positive energy and prosperity are represented in the painting of a waterfall. Waterfalls are strong yet they have a calming effect.

Water play can accompany the story or extend the story.

Engaging the Child with Challenges in the Drawing, Writing, Reading Process

As a parent or teacher we can be proactive rather than reactive. We can prepare the environment ahead of time in order to minimize distractions and engage the child in the reading process.

Prior to beginning to read the story, think about how each child learns best. Is the child an auditory learner, a visual learner, a tactile/kinesthetic learner? What is the child's interests? What seems to distract him/her? Once you know the child's strengths incorporate them into the story process.

The following ideas encompass all types of learning modalities and styles. The ideas/strategies are universally designed to provide a framework for engaging the child in the story telling and reading process as **an active** participant.

A child who is a **visual learner** understands best when they see information. They may be challenged when trying to understand spoken instructions. Visual students like diagrams, pictorial essays, and a visual chart of the daily routine accompanied by a visual menu of directions. Visual learners notice small details. They like to read, draw and do crafts. They will watch a situation before getting involved. Visual learners express themselves through creativity. Visual learners have a strong imagination and learn best when they write things down. Using a wipe off board during the story may help to focus the child who is a visual learner. They like colors so focusing on the illustrations in the story will help to sustain attention to the story. They may also like to be looking at a person who is speaking because it helps them focus. Guide the visual learner in looking at the headings and pictures before reading whole sentences. Highlight important words in color. Connect new information with concepts that he/she already knows so he/she can understand topics as a whole. Brainstorm together, use diagrams and mind maps to show how everything you are learning fits together. Use different forms of technology to present the story such as a power point presentation or pictures on your Ipad. Let him/her be creative and use their imagination. After reading the story, ask him/her to close their eyes so they can picture what they have just learned.

The child who is a **tactile/kinesthetic learner** processes information best when they experience the story by touching and moving. Add sound to the story, whistle like the hummingbird or tap your feet as the little girl in the story walks over the bridge. Children who learn best by touching and moving are often considered hyperactive because they get bored and begin to fidget. They show excitement and interest by moving around. They enjoy exploring and find it easier to understand abstract topics if they are explained using practical examples. The tactile/kinesthetic learner often talks fast and uses his/her hands, using touch, space and movement to learn. To engage this type of learner incorporate sign language into the story reading or use role playing. Sometimes sitting in a weighted chair or a bean bag chair provides the child with sensory feedback while the story is being read.

Some strategies that will help the tactile/kinesthetic learner are:

- Use music as the story is told. Take short breaks.

- Use visual images by having the child close his/her eyes and see the image in his/her mind.

- Make games, and puzzles from "A River's Journey".

- Role-play or demonstrate the information contained in the story.

- Have the child re-teach the story to others using a puppet as a prop.

- Allow the child to lie on his/her back while listening or reading.

Sometimes it is beneficial to place the challenging child in a "position of importance" for the story sharing such as being the birch tree that waits while the butterfly approaches its, trunk. Or perhaps anticipating carrying flowers to the river's ridge as that part is read. This encourages delayed self-gratification and impulse control. Positive affirmation statements also work wonders to help a child "stay on task".

In summary, when teaching all learners, it's helpful to stand or move while learning. Allow frequent short breaks. Teach with real life objects. Dress in costume. Be animated and use voice inflection while reading. Sing and dance perhaps like the dandelion in the story!

Embrace the child's idiosyncrasies and energy and channel them in a positive direction.

Unit Plan Ideas/Themes

You can extend the child's learning utilizing a multi-modality approach. This approach allows the child to use all of his/her senses to reinforce the concepts present in the story, "A River's Journey". Children are sensory learners. They need to see, hear, touch, and move in order to learn best. The following ideas relate to the content reflected in the story as well as the art work that is displayed. I hope it inspires you to "make learning come alive" for the children whose lives you touch every day!

ART:

Extend your child's curiosity for exploration and nature by implementing some of these fun "nature based" art ideas:

- making a bird's nest from things found in nature
- create insects using objects from nature such as leaves & twigs
- make leaf sun catchers
- find or create mud prints
- feather painting
- painting rocks
- shadow tracings with objects from the outdoors
- a nature diorama

MUSIC:

Connect the story content in "A River's Journey" to songs that reflect the river's travels in the story. Some examples might be:

Songs about the River:

- When I Sail on the River

- The River Song by 2 Little Rockers

Songs about the heart:

- A Little Wheel Turning in My Heart.

- This Little Heart of Mine.

Songs about the sun:

- Mr. Golden Sun (Please Shine Down on Me)

- You are My Sunshine

Songs about Birds and Flowers:

- Bird Songs and Rhymes from DLTK's Crafts for kids

- Bird Songs and Fingerplays from StepByStepc.com

- Free Bird Sounds, Songs, Rhymes for Circle Time -LivingMomtessoriNow.com

DRAMA:

After reading the story, "A River's Journey", allow the children to role play and act out the components of the story. Younger children can use puppets to re-tell the story. The older children can write a play or a skit about the various content in the story and re-enact it.

Perhaps you can include the following props in the children's play/skit:

- Trees, flowers, birds, a heart ,the sun, a lady bug, a caterpillar, stars, ice, snow, a bridge, rainbows, and a humming bird.

Encourage children to continue to read and re-enact the components of the stories that they read.

SCIENCE:

Children learn best through scientific inquiry. Scientific Inquiry refers to the method by which children look at nature in an evidence-based manner. Scientific inquiry develops the child's ability to question what he/she reads in a critical way.

Scientific inquiry helps children to develop critical thinking skills and to wonder about the world around them like a scientist would.

You can promote inquiry-based learning using the contents in the story, "A River's Journey", by asking children to think about what they know about the river, what they want to learn about the river, and upon completion of the story reading, what they have learned about the river. This is called the KWL approach. When children are encouraged to interact with the world in a scientific way, they find themselves observing, questioning, hypothesizing, predicting, investigating, interpreting, and communicating. Inquiry-based learning helps children make their own connections about what they learn.

Provide the child (the little scientist) with a magnifying glass in order to observe nature, a net to collect insects in and a jar to collect things found in nature for further discovery. Give the child a memo pad to write or draw their investigations and discoveries.

You can encourage the children to become little scientists and "think outside of the box". Sometimes sharing some interesting facts about the content in the story can become a spring board for increased discovery and curiosity. Some examples might be discussing ladybug facts: ladybugs aren't bugs at all they are beetles. Each ladybug looks different. Ladybugs eat their own eggs. Ladybugs smell with their feet.

You can peak the child's curiosity about butterflies by asking "Do you know" questions, such as "Do you know that butterflies can't fly if they're cold.?" "Do you know that butterfly wings are actually transparent.?" Or you can share interesting and thought provoking facts about the butterfly that would be of interest to young children, for example, butterflies taste with their feet. Butterflies drink from mud puddles.

And of course you can explore the cardinal's life that is presented early in the story: " A bright red cardinal balances on a branch in the breeze. How does he stay on with such ease?"

Some science experiments/investigations following the story reading might include child-based explorations regarding:

- How fast a river flows.

- The contents of a river- what is it made of?

- The sun's gravitational force.

- Vegetation that grows on the river banks.

- Animals and insects that live in the river.

- Electricity.

- Balance.

- The life of : humming birds, lady bugs, cardinals, doves, caterpillars, butterflies, dandelions.

- Trees, rainbows, stars, fire.

- The four seasons.

- The river current.

- Where does the river go?

HISTORY:

As an extension to the story, "A River's Journey", you can explore the history of local rivers and their importance. The two local river's, near where the story was written, are the Hudson River and the Mohawk River in New York State.

You can peak children's curiosity, and perhaps instill a passion for history. As an extension to the story, share with the older children some interesting aspects of history regarding the rivers nearby where they live. Some key points of interest, about the Hudson River, are:

- Henry Hudson discovered and explored the Hudson River in September 1609.

- The river is located in the United States of America and in New York State.

- It is 315 miles long and 202 feet deep.

- The Hudson River flows through two states in the United States, New York and New Jersey.

- The Hudson River is home to many different types of fish : catfish, striped bass and yellow perch.

- An emergency airplane landing, known as the Miracle on the Hudson, took place on the river and saved all 155 passengers and crew on January 15, 2009.

The Mohawk River is a branch of the Hudson *River*. The *Mohawk* River flows into the Hudson River in Cohoes, New York, just north of the city of Albany.

Some thought -provoking facts about this river, that older children can explore further, are:

- The river has been important to transportation to the west as it passes through the Appalachian Mountains, between the Catskill Mountains and the Adirondack Mountains to the north.

- The river was named after the Mohawk Native American tribe.

- The Mohawk tribes lived in the eastern part of New York, parts of Cananda, and Vermont.

- The Mohawk were part of four Iroquois people that worked with the British during the American Revolutionary War. They wanted to prevent colonists from taking their land in the Mohawk Valley.

The historical ideas presented here are personally meaningful. They provide ideas for endless historical explorations and discoveries as an extension to reading, "A River's Journey".

FAITH:

The story of the river's journey lends itself to lessons in spirituality, hope, faith, and resilience.

As the author, I chose a story about the river because a river symbolizes life, freedom, and the passage of time. Rivers are strong, ever flowing, and resilient.

I often say, to my friends, and to people that I meet, "I am so glad that on my journey through life that you were on my path." Life is a journey and we need to keep moving forward, remain strong, and maintain a positive attitude even in the face of adversity.

Life is like a river, it is always moving, it can move slowly or it can move quickly. It can change course but nothing can stop the river from flowing. The same happens with life, there are no external circumstances that can stop it from flowing forward. If the river finds an obstacle in its way, the river water's strength removes it from its path or finds an alternative path to move ahead. So to is life, with strength, conviction, and faith we can move mountains.

YOU CAN MOVE MOUNTAINS

NANCY T. CUPOLO

The painting of the mountains, completed by my daughter Lisa, is not contained in the story, "A River's Journey". I share it with you as an illustration of how a faith- based lesson can emerge from the story itself.

Mountains, as well as many of the paintings in the story, demonstrate the power of nature. Mountains symbolize escape, freedom and conquest. Mountains also are known to symbolize spirituality and closeness to God.

The Mountain Spirit (Sanshin), Korea's most important deity, demonstrates a veneration of mountains. The Mountain Spirit is considered a protector of Buddhism. Korean Buddhist temples include a shrine dedicated to him.

In Catholicism mountains were the places where the prophets went to be closer to God and discern his will at times of crisis. After the arrival of the children of Israel, at the foot of Mount Sinai, Moses went to the mountain and returned with stone tablets containing the Ten Commandments.

Discussing with children the path of life, using the river as a focal point, can become a faith -filled lesson. It is believed in some religions that the river is a living water that represents the spirit and power that was given to followers of faith and religion. The spirit's presence points to the cleansing and sanctifying strength in the hearts of God's children.

The Jordan River runs along the border between Jordan, the Palestinian West Bank, Israel and southwestern Syria. The river has significance in Judaism and Christianity. According to the Bible, the Israelites crossed it into the Promised Land and Jesus of Nazareth was baptized by John the Baptist in it. This could become a springboard for discussion in one's faith.

The river represents the never-ending flow of God's grace. It is believed to bring healing and nourishment. The river's spiritual meaning perhaps represents how life is always changing just like the river, and that we must learn to let go and let God.

As a springboard for further discovery you might ask yourself: "What do the mountains and the river mean to me spiritually?".

Symbolism in Art

Throughout the story, "A River's Journey", the illustrator has beautifully captured the joy that nature provides to us in several unique ways. As the child's first teacher, you can incorporate the symbolic meaning of the paintings into a discussion in order to highlight the key components of the story. You may also use the symbolism outlined below to encourage the child to persevere; remain hopeful and strong throughout his/her life.

DANDELIONS

With their golden flowers in the early spring, dandelions represent the return of life, the rebirth of growth and green after a harsh winter. They display an abundance of strength and power.

TREES

Throughout art, trees have been utilized as symbols of growth, seasonal death, and revival. The tree's leaves change color, wither and die yet they return to their beautiful splendor. The Tree of

Life, the Sacred Tree, and the Tree of Knowledge are often mentioned in stories. Birch trees represent new beginnings.

SUNSHINE

The sun represents energy, power, and positivity,

BUTTERFLIES

The butterfly is a symbol of transformation and hope; across cultures, it has become a symbol for rebirth and resurrection, a triumph of the spirit.

WINTER

The cold and darkness of winter often symbolizes a time to hibernate and rest. While winter can be lonely and represent despair, it's also the season before spring, a time of new beginnings, hope, and joy.

WINTER INTO SPRING

OCEAN

The ocean is the beginning of life on earth, and it symbolizes stability because it has remained unchanged for centuries.

A RAINBOW

A rainbow is often a sign of hope, the beauty after the storm, a pot of gold and good fortune at the rainbow's end. For many, a rainbow represents inclusivity and diversity. It is seen as an all-embracing image of love and friendship.

FLOWERS

With their colorful and beautiful blooms, flowers are often seen as symbols of joy and pleasure. Some flowers are seen as symbols of friendship and purity, while others are symbols of forgiveness.

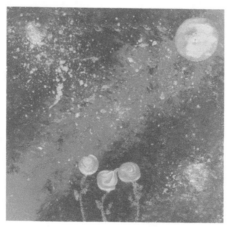

DOVES

Doves, usually white in color, are used in many settings as symbols of peace, freedom, or love.

The dove has been a symbol of peace and innocence for thousands of years in many different cultures.

WATERFALL

Water symbolizes a flow of positivity, and prosperity. Water-falls are said to symbolize the process of letting go, cleansing and the continuous flow of energy and life.

SHOOTING STAR

A shooting star is a symbol of hope, and a chance to wish for a brighter future.

Story Facts about A River That Will Help to Peak a Child's Curiosity

A story never truly ends. It remains in our hearts and minds forever. It becomes a base for future learning.

In the story, "A River's Journey", there are several facts about the river that emerge as the reader reviews the contents of the book. Some examples are:

- The river flows swift and fast.

- The river is made of rain and snow.

- The river travels around a bend.

- There is beauty on each river bank side.

- The river's path is both shallow and deep.

- The river basin churns.

- There is a river ridge.

- The river twists and turns.

- The flashy river flows steadily both night and day.

- The river's current continues on it's way.

- The river does empty into the sea.

Hopefully the reader, no matter how young or old, will be inspired to learn as much as he/she can about the river.

The following additional facts, about the river, can assist the reader with continued discovery that links learning to previous information. This is called *scaffolding or linked learning*. It is an extremely beneficial teaching strategy for young children.

Connecting prior knowledge to current knowledge creates bridges for learning that connects new knowledge with what the child already knows. This creates a "mental link" that makes the acquisition of learning easier.

Prior knowledge refers to the information that a learner has at the beginning of learning a new topic/concept. The following river facts should help "link" learning, what the child already knows, to new concepts in a straightforward and easy fashion depending upon the child's developmental age and interest.

Some facts to contemplate in order to encourage further discovery are:

- The water, flowing through a river, usually flows into the ocean or a lake. Rivers are created from rain and snow. Rivers are an important part of the water cycle.

- Long ago the river was the main mode of transportation. Rivers provide travel routes for exploration, commerce and recreation. River valleys and plains provide fertile soils. Farmers in dry regions irrigate their crops by using water carried by irrigation ditches from nearby rivers. Rivers are an important energy source.

✳ Rivers are like roads. They carry water and nutrients to many areas. They also help drain rainwater and provide habitats for many species of plants and animals. Rivers help to shape the features of the earth.

✳ A river is actually a wide natural stream of freshwater that flows into an ocean. The river is formed by smaller streams, called tributaries that enter it along its course. Rivers constantly change according to the water flow.

Some additional tidbits of information that you may want to discuss with older children include:

✳ Rivers can flood if there is a lot of rainfall.

✳ The start of a river is called the source. The end of a river is called a mouth.

✳ The longest river in the world is the River Nile.

✳ Rivers can be all kinds of colors, not just blue; rivers can be clear or muddy brown too.

✳ Rivers are the source of freshwater which is essential for the survival of all living beings.

The flowing water of a river is used to generate electricity. Hydro power is a clean energy source.

The river contains several life forms such as algae, plants, zooplankton, crayfish, insects, mussels, fish, reptiles, turtles, ducks, otters, crocodiles, catfish, dragonfly and crabs.

A river has Oxbow Lakes. Oxbow lakes are pools of water formed by meanders, the curves found in the river.

You can extend the child's thinking, and desire for further discovery and learning, by sharing just a few facts, then let them become little explorers and discover the rest!

Conclusion

It is that look of wonder on the child's face, that insatiable curiosity evident in the child's eyes, that expressed desire to explore further, that we, as the child's first teacher, strive for.

If we can foster wonder, curiosity, and exploration, through story-telling, drawing, writing, and reading early in life the child will become an enthusiastic life-long learner!

"Lessons of Hope & Resilience: A Parent/Teacher Guide" for the story "A River's Journey" provides you with the strategies that will foster a child's innate curiosity and wonder for a life time!

Acknowledgements:

I would like to acknowledge Jessika Hazelton, from the Troy Book Makers Publishing Company, for her enthusiasm, encouragement, editing expertise, and patience throughout the production of this book.

I am grateful for the continued support of my family for all of my publications, in particular, Frank, my husband, Lisa and Andria, my daughters, and my seven siblings as well as my extended family and friends.

References

Britannica, The Editors of Encyclopedia. (2019) *Mohawk River, Encyclopedia Britannica*, https://www.britannica.com/place/Mohawk-River.

Brunn, Peter, (2010) *The Lesson Planning Handbook Essential Strategies That Inspire Student Thinking & Learning*, Scholastic Books.

Christopher, Ian, (2020) *The Social Emotional Learning of Children is at Stake*, Age of Awareness Newsletter.

Cudmore, Bob, (2015) *Lost Mohawk Valley*, The History Press.

Fisher, Andrew, (2010) *Shadow Tribe, The Making of Columbia River Indian Identity*, University of Washington Press.

Gear, W. Michael and Gear, Kathleen O'Neal, (1914) *People of the River*, Tor Books.

Locker, Thomas, (1993) *Where the River Begins*, Picture Puffin Books.

Martin, Marc, (2015) *A River*, Google Books.

Mc Daniel, Jay,(2021) *The Spirituality of Rivers, Rivers as Spiritual Guides, Two Essays*, https://www.openhorizons.org.

McDaniel, Jay, B., (1989) *Of God and Pelicans*, Westminster/John Knox Press.

Talbott, Hudson (2009) *River of Dreams: The Story of the Hudson River*, G.P. Putnam's and Sons.

https://www.srmt-nsn.gov culture and history

https://www.allaboutheaven.org

https://www.theexplanation.com

https://symbolismandmetaphor.com

https://www.factsjustforkids.com

https://justfunfacts.com

https://www.newyorkalmanack.com 2022

About the Author:

Nancy T. Cupolo, Professor Emeritus, has conducted thousands of seminars for parents, educators, and administrators on topics relating to young children. She has a keen sense of being able to see the world through the eyes of the child. Nancy started her career as a teacher of children with special needs. She served as an Assistant with the New York State Education Department prior to operating her own pre-school.

Professor Emeritus Cupolo was an active advocate for children, as a faculty member and as the Department Chairperson, within the Teacher Education Department at Hudson Valley Community College in Troy, New York. She is the recipient of several recognitions and awards including the *State of New York Chancellor's Award for Excellence in Teaching*, and a *Life Time Achievement Award* for her passion for teaching and dedication to the children within her community.

She is the author of two books, "A River's Journey", (2022), an imaginative and beautifully illustrated story about the magic of nature from the river's view, and "Through the Child's Eyes: Looking at Life Through the Lens of a Child, A Parenting Cookbook for Success" (2023).

Most importantly Nancy is the parent of two grown children and she was raised in a family of nine children. Currently she has her own consulting business titled, "Children First: Educational and Behavioral Consultation Services".

About the Illustrator:

Lisa M. Cupolo, owner and creator of Intuitive Arts, started painting during the pandemic in January 2022 after her father gifted her a set of paints during the 2021 Christmas holidays. She quickly realized that she had a passion for painting and the arts. Lisa uses her intuition to paint.

Lisa is the Illustrator of two books, "A River's Journey" (2022), and "Through the Child's Eyes, Looking at Life Through the Lens of a Child , A Parenting Cookbook for Success".(2023)

www.intuitiveartsbylisa.com